THE HANDWRITING PRACTICE FOR ADULTS

PRINT AND CURSIVE
WRITING WORKBOOK

Dreamers inherit the future`s promise.

Dreamers inherit the future's promise.

IMPROVE YOUR PENMANSHIP WITH

ALPHABET TRACKING INSPIRATIONAL WORDS, MOTIVATIONAL QUOTES AND SHORT POEMS

THIS BOOK BELONGS TO:

Thank You!

Thank you for your purchase.
We have loved creating this book
and we hope you get hours
of handwriting practice.

We value your feedback and opinion
as it assists with our next creation.
You also help other buyers - just like you,
make the right decision.

You might also like

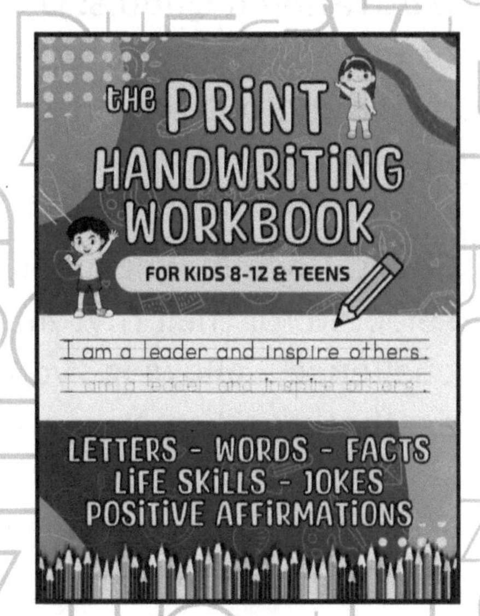

INTRODUCTION

Welcome to **"Handwriting Practice for Adults,"** the comprehensive guide designed specifically for adults looking to improve their handwriting in both print and cursive styles. Tailored to meet the needs and interests of an adult audience, this book serves as a multifaceted tool for enhancing handwriting skills while engaging with thought-provoking and inspiring content.

Within these pages, you will encounter a variety of sections, each meticulously crafted to support your handwriting journey:

Alphabet Mastery: Begin with the basics by exploring exercises focused on the alphabet in both print and cursive formats. This foundational section includes detailed guides on letter formation, ensuring a strong base for further development.

Inspirational Words: Progress to tracing and copying inspirational words that not only serve to practice your handwriting but also to motivate and uplift your spirit. This section is designed to enhance your lexical range while embedding positive messages into your practice.

Motivational Quotes: Dive deeper into the art of handwriting with a collection of motivational quotes. Here, you'll have the opportunity to refine your skills by writing out powerful and stirring quotations that encourage reflection and inspiration.

Short Poems: Engage with the beauty of language through short poems selected for their rhythmic and thematic richness. This segment offers a unique challenge, allowing you to practice handwriting while appreciating the aesthetic and emotional depth of poetry.

This book is more than a handwriting practice workbook; it's a journey towards self-improvement and personal growth. By integrating elements of motivation, inspiration, and the beauty of language, **"Handwriting Practice for Adults"** aims to provide a fulfilling and enriching experience. Whether you're looking to polish your handwriting for professional reasons or simply wish to embark on a personal development project, this guide is your companion for a journey of exploration and improvement.

UPPERCASE LETTERS

A A B B C C D D E E

F F G G H H I I J J

K K L L M M N N O O

P P Q Q R R S S T T

U U V V W W X X Y Y

Z Z

LOWERCASE LETTERS

a a b b c c d d e e

f f g g h h i i j j

k k l l m m n n o o

p p q q r r s s t t

u u v v w w x x y y

z z

Part I
Letters

Track the dotted letters and then write the letters on your own.

A B C D E F G H I J K L M N O P Q R S T U V W X Y Z

1 2 3 A A A A A A A A A A

1 2 a a a a a a a a a a a

A A A A A A A A A A

a a a a a a a a a a a a

A B C D E F G H I J K L M N O P Q R S T U V W X Y Z

B B B B B B B B B B

b b b b b b b b b b b

B B B B B B B B B B B

b b b b b b b b b b b b

A B C D E F G H I J K L M N O P Q R S T U V W X Y Z

C C C C C C C C C C

c c c c c c c c c c c

C C C C C C C C C C C C

c c c c c c c c c c c c c

A B C D E F G H I J K L M N O P Q R S T U V W X Y Z

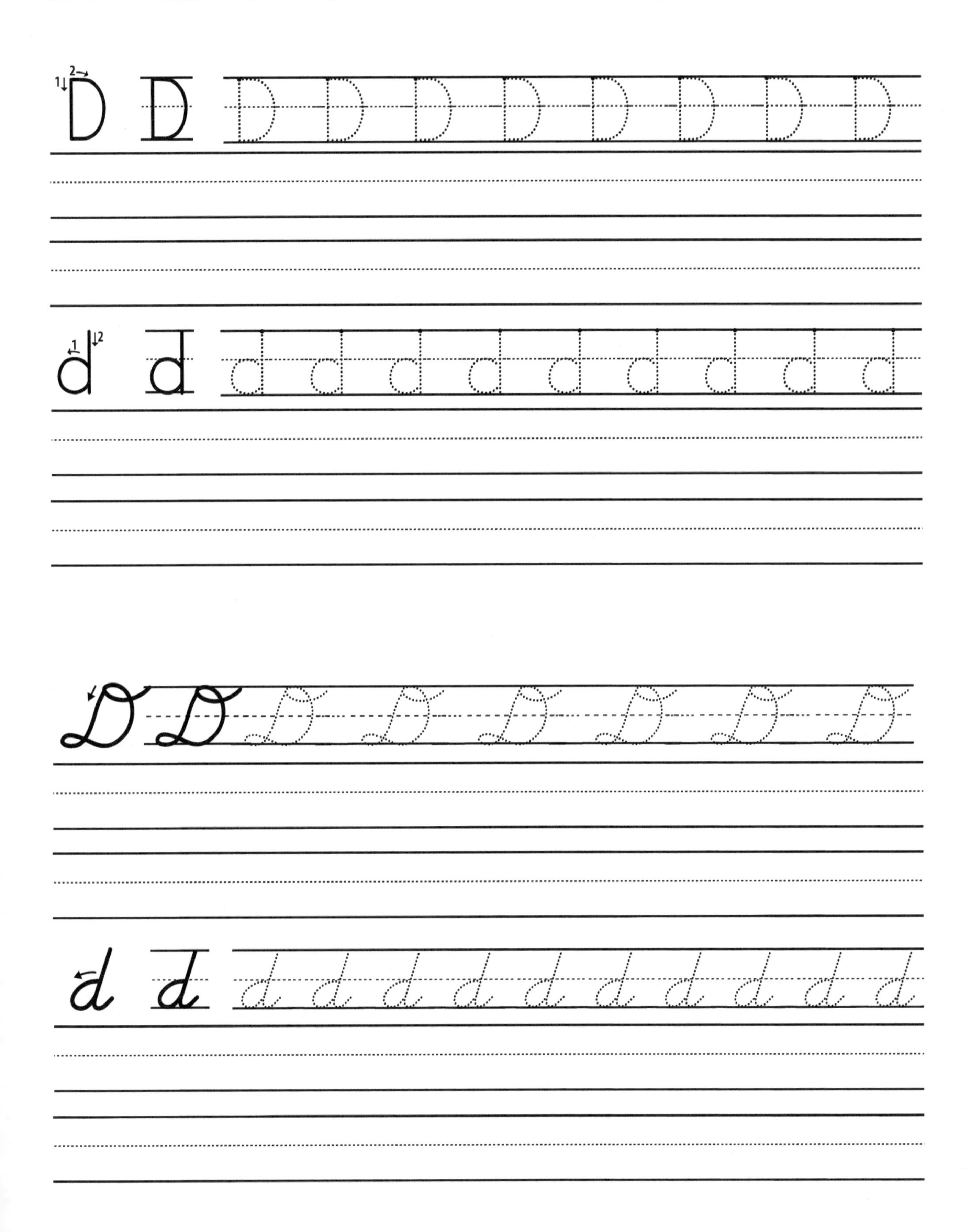

A B C D E F G H I J K L M N O P Q R S T U V W X Y Z

E E E E E E E E E E E

e e e e e e e e e e e

ℰ ℰ ℰ ℰ ℰ ℰ ℰ ℰ ℰ ℰ ℰ

e e e e e e e e e e e e e

A B C D E **F** G H I J K L M N O P Q R S T U V W X Y Z

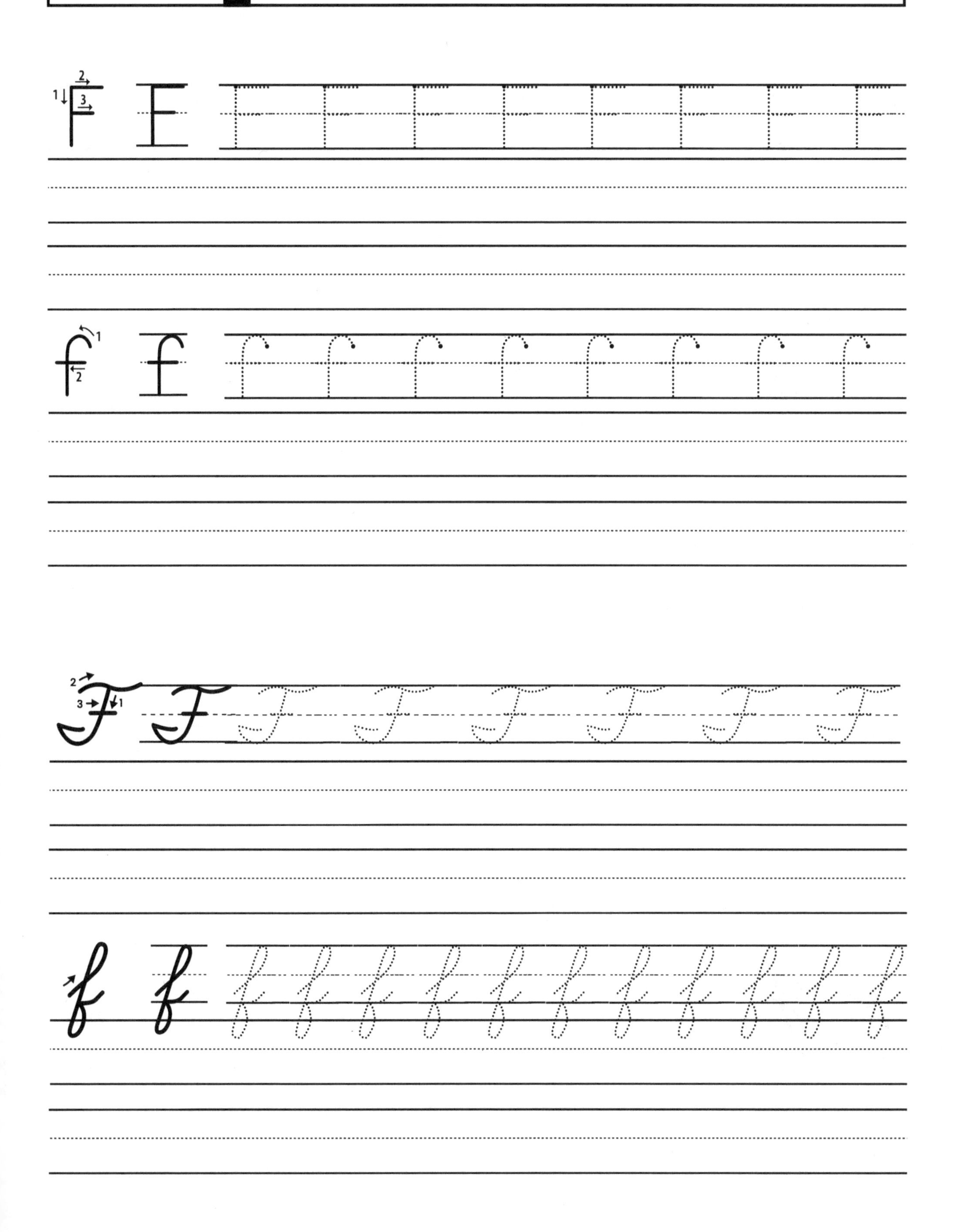

A B C D E F **G** H I J K L M N O P Q R S T U V W X Y Z

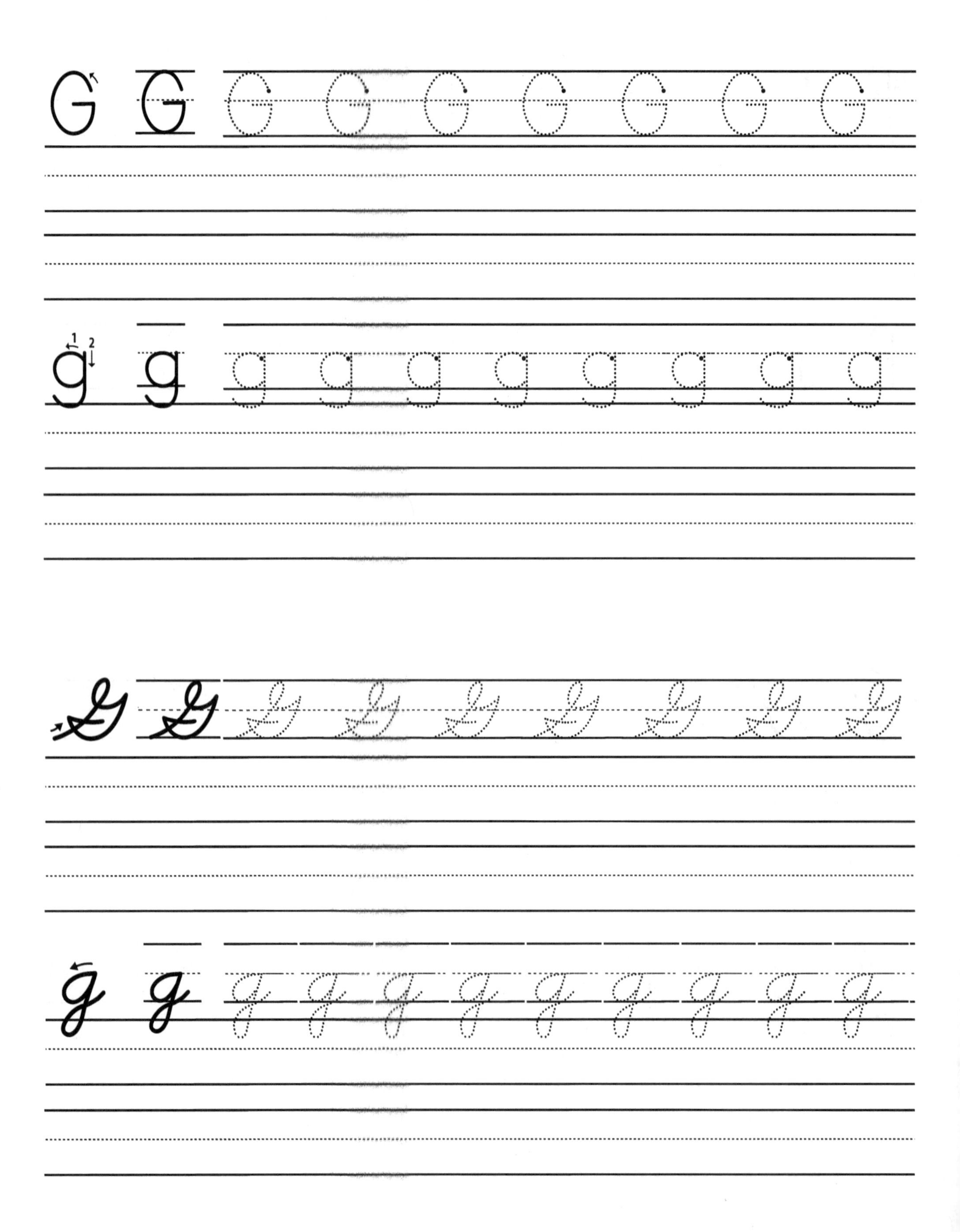

A B C D E F G **H** I J K L M N O P Q R S T U V W X Y Z

H H H H H H H H H

h h h h h h h h h h

H H H H H H H H H H

h h h h h h h h h h h

A B C D E F G H **I** J K L M N O P Q R S T U V W X Y Z

I I

i i

I I

i i

A B C D E F G H I **J** K L M N O P Q R S T U V W X Y Z

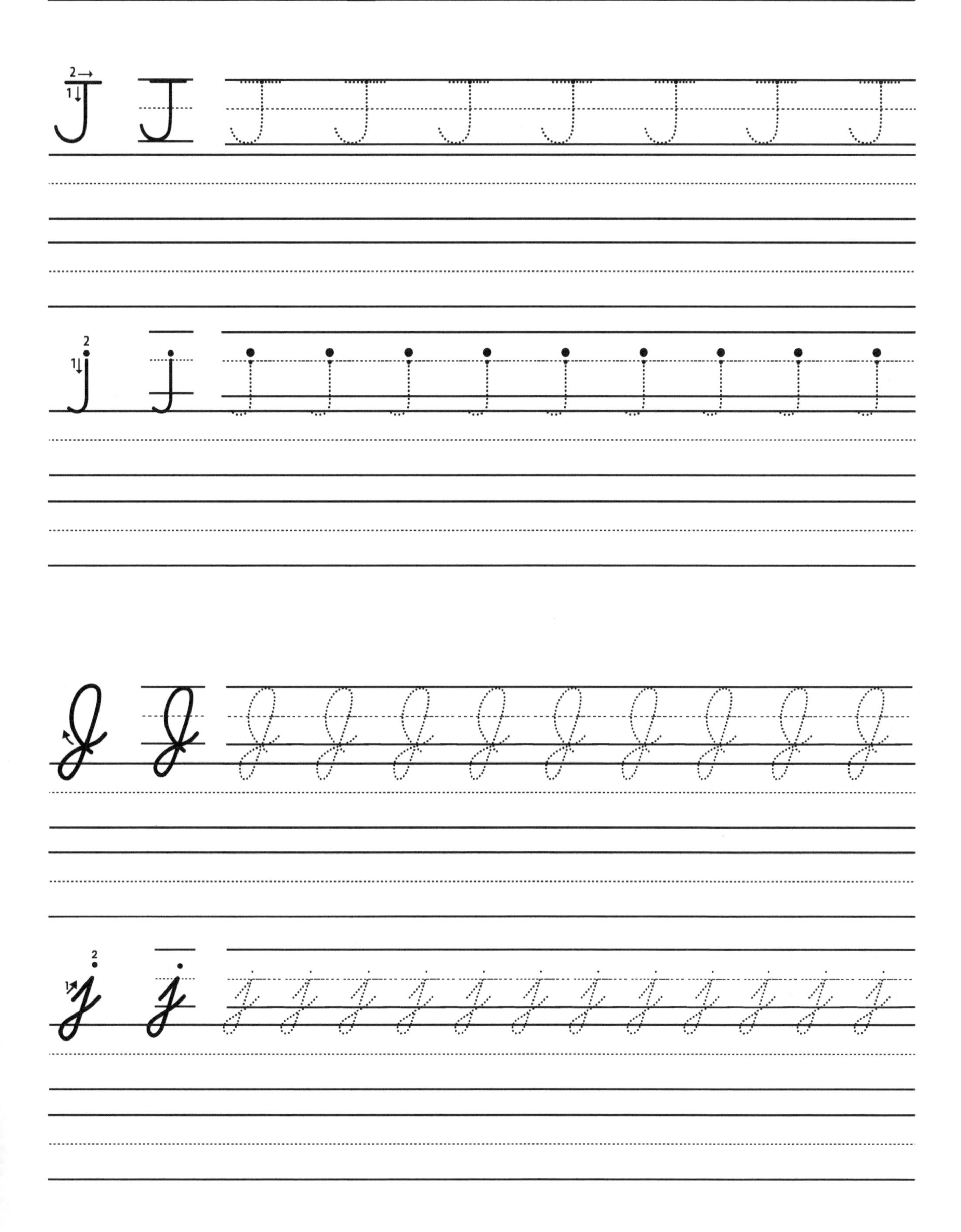

A B C D E F G H I J K L M N O P Q R S T U V W X Y Z

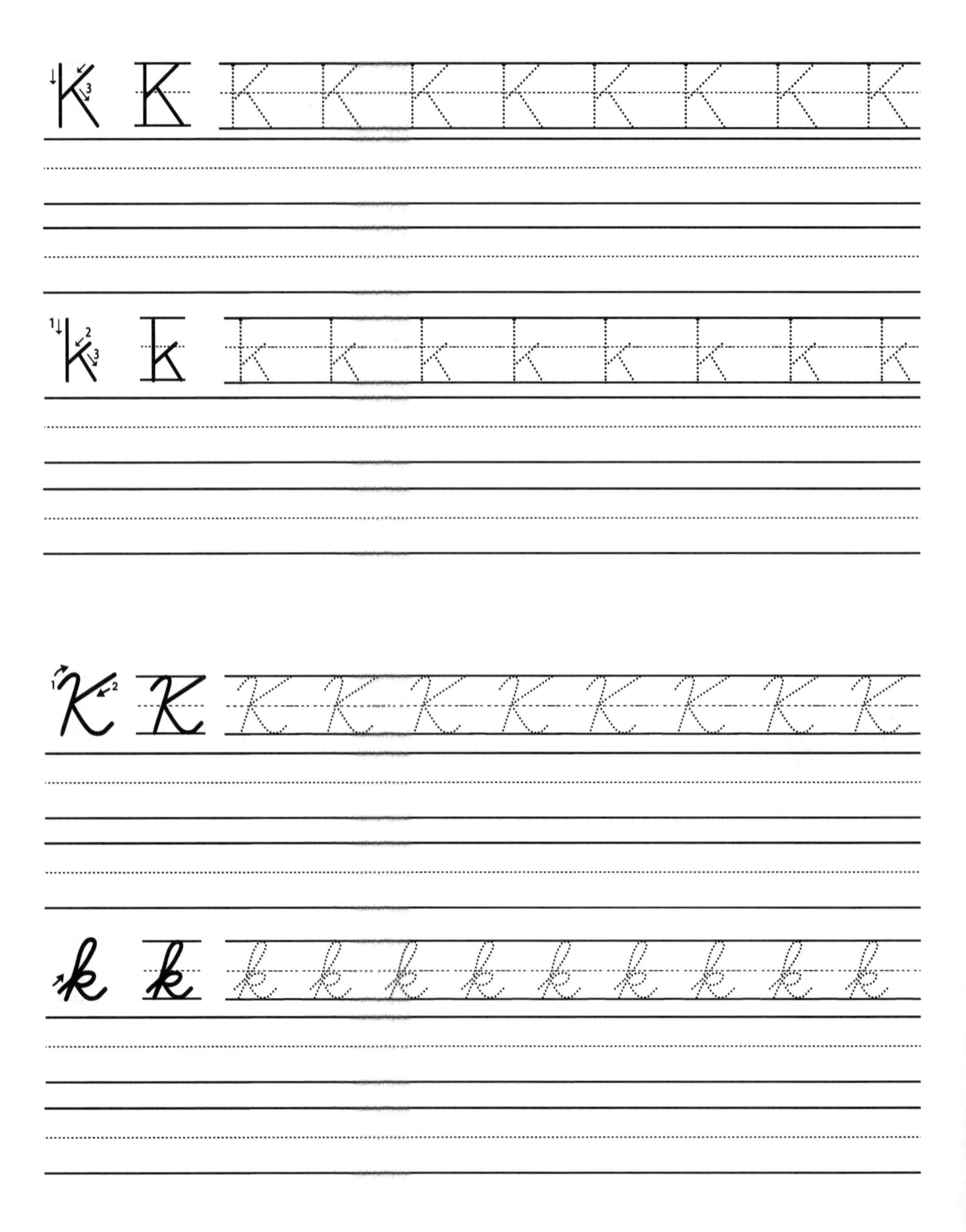

A B C D E F G H I J K L M N O P Q R S T U V W X Y Z

L L

l l

𝓛 𝓛

𝓁 𝓁

A B C D E F G H I J K L **M** N O P Q R S T U V W X Y Z

M M M M M M M M M

m m m m m m m m m

M M M M M M M M M

m m m m m m m m m

A B C D E F G H I J K L M **N** O P Q R S T U V W X Y Z

N N N N N N N N N N

n n n n n n n n n n n

N N N N N N N N N N N

n n n n n n n n n n n

A B C D E F G H I J K L M N O P Q R S T U V W X Y Z

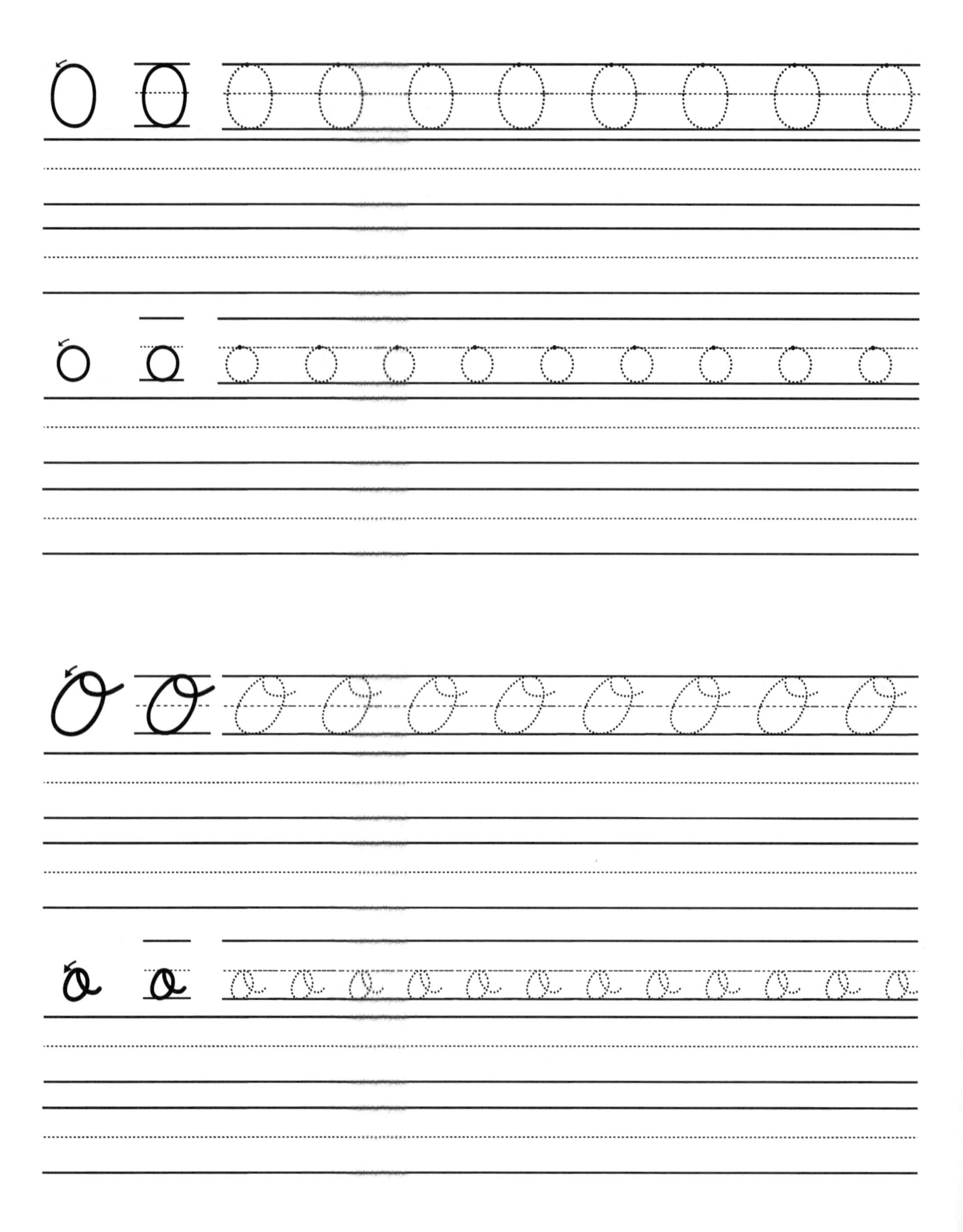

A B C D E F G H I J K L M N O **P** Q R S T U V W X Y Z

P P P P P P P P P P P

p p p p p p p p p p

P P P P P P P P P P P

p p p p p p p p p p p p

A B C D E F G H I J K L M N O P Q R S T U V W X Y Z

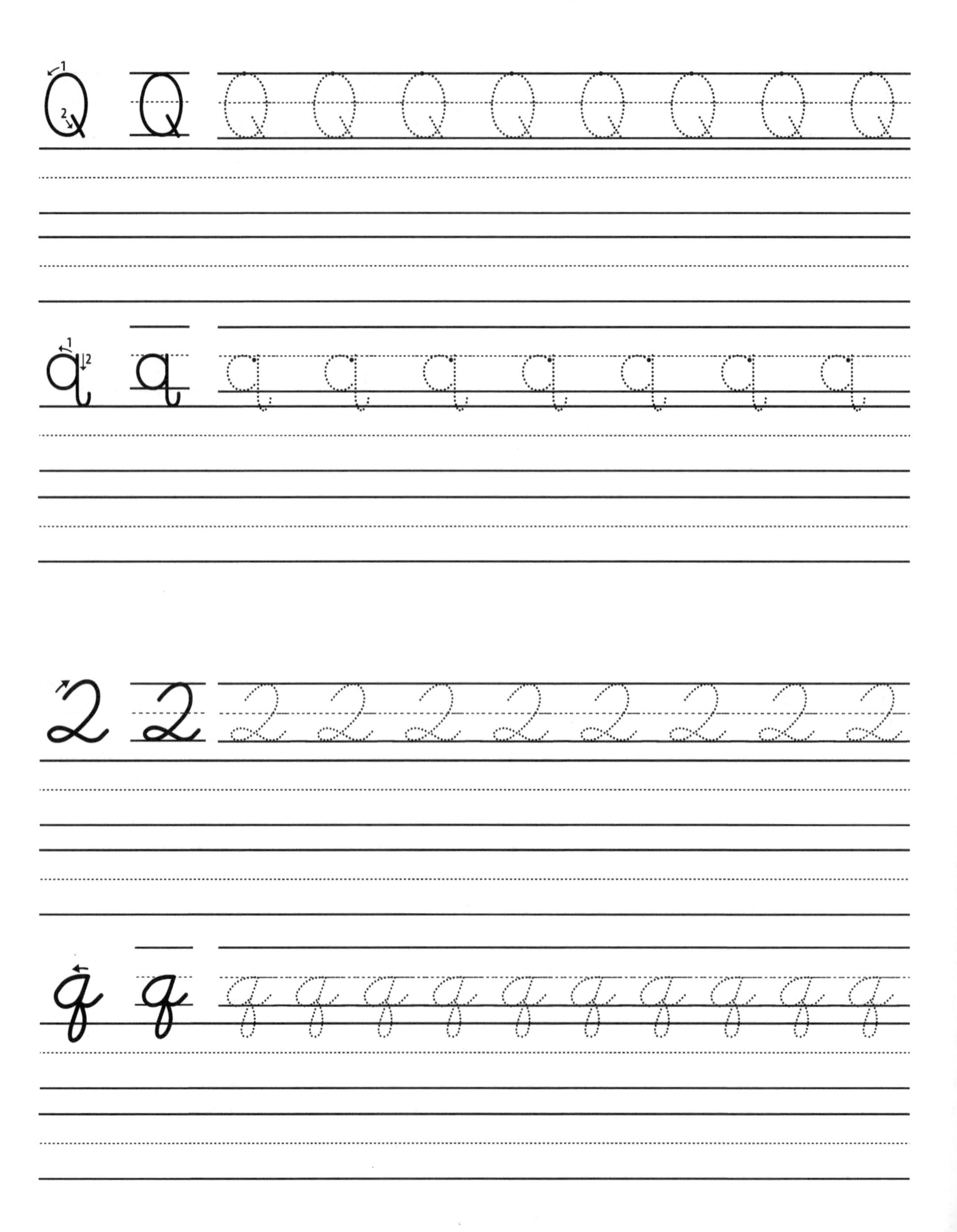

A B C D E F G H I J K L M N O P Q **R** S T U V W X Y Z

R R R R R R R R R R R

r r r r r r r r r r r r

R R R R R R R R R R

r r r r r r r r r r r r r r

A B C D E F G H I J K L M N O P Q R **S** T U V W X Y Z

S S S S S S S S S S

s s s s s s s s s s

𝒮 𝒮 𝒮 𝒮 𝒮 𝒮 𝒮 𝒮 𝒮

𝓈 𝓈 𝓈 𝓈 𝓈 𝓈 𝓈 𝓈 𝓈 𝓈 𝓈 𝓈 𝓈 𝓈

A B C D E F G H I J K L M N O P Q R S **T** U V W X Y Z

T T

t t

T T

t t

A B C D E F G H I J K L M N O P Q R S T U V W X Y Z

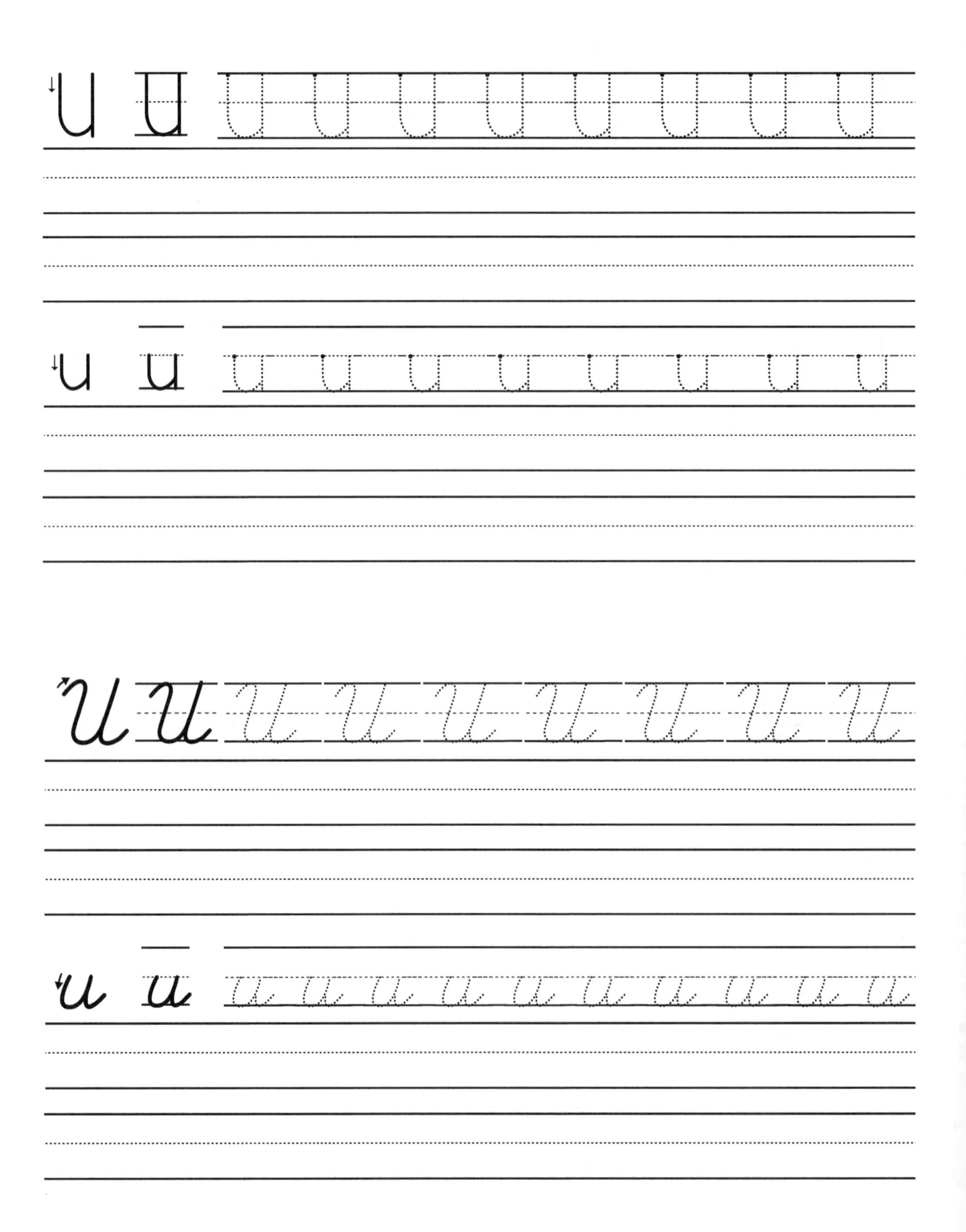

A B C D E F G H I J K L M N O P Q R S T U **V** W X Y Z

V V

v v

V V

v v

A B C D E F G H I J K L M N O P Q R S T U V **W** X Y Z

W W W W W W W W

w w w w w w w w w

W W W W W W W W

w w w w w w w w w

A B C D E F G H I J K L M N O P Q R S T U V W **X** Y Z

X X X X X X X X X X X

x x x x x x x x x x

𝒳 𝒳 𝒳 𝒳 𝒳 𝒳 𝒳 𝒳 𝒳 𝒳

𝓍 𝓍 𝓍 𝓍 𝓍 𝓍 𝓍 𝓍 𝓍 𝓍

A B C D E F G H I J K L M N O P Q R S T U V W X **Y** Z

Y Y

y y

Y Y

y y

A B C D E F G H I J K L M N O P Q R S T U V W X Y **Z**

Z Z

z z

Z Z

z z

Part 2
Inspirational Words

Track the dotted words and then write the words on your own.

Aspire Aspire

Aspire *Aspire*

Brave Brave

Brave *Brave*

Courage Courage

Courage *Courage*

Dream Dream

Dream *Dream*

Empower Empower

Empower *Empower*

Freedom Freedom

Freedom *Freedom*

Grow Grow

Grow *Grow*

Hope Hope

Hope *Hope*

Inspire Inspire

Inspire *Inspire*

Joy Joy

Joy *Joy*

Kindness Kindness

Kindness *Kindness*

Love Love

Love *Love*

Motivate Motivate

Motivate *Motivate*

Nurture Nurture

Nurture *Nurture*

Overcome Overcome

Overcome *Overcome*

Persevere Persevere

Persevere *Persevere*

Quest Quest

Quest *Quest*

Rise Rise

Rise *Rise*

Strength Strength

Strength *Strength*

Thrive Thrive

Thrive *Thrive*

Unite Unite

Unite *Unite*

Valor Valor

Valor *Valor*

Wisdom Wisdom

Wisdom *Wisdom*

eXcel eXcel

eXcel *eXcel*

Yield Yield

Yield *Yield*

Zeal Zeal

Zeal *Zeal*

Part 3
Motivation Quotes

Track the dotted quotes and then write the quotes on your own.

Believe in yourself; there`s more inside you.

Believe in yourself; there`s more inside you.

Believe in yourself; there's more inside you.

Believe in yourself; there's more inside you.

Love what you do to achieve greatness.

Love what you do to achieve greatness.

Love what you do to achieve greatness.

Love what you do to achieve greatness.

Hardships forge paths to extraordinary ends.

Hardships forge paths to extraordinary ends.

Hardships forge paths to extraordinary ends.

Hardships forge paths to extraordinary ends.

Dreamers inherit the future`s promise.

Dreamers inherit the future`s promise.

Dreamers inherit the future's promise.

Dreamers inherit the future's promise.

Success hinges on courage, not outcomes.

Success hinges on courage, not outcomes.

Success hinges on courage, not outcomes.

Success hinges on courage, not outcomes.

Keep moving; time waits for no one.

Keep moving; time waits for no one.

Keep moving; time waits for no one.

Keep moving; time waits for no one.

Your actions ripple through the world.

Your actions ripple through the world.

Your actions ripple through the world.

Your actions ripple through the world.

Our glory lies in rising after falls.

Our glory lies in rising after falls.

Our glory lies in rising after falls.

Our glory lies in rising after falls.

Nothing`s impossible until it`s achieved.

Nothing`s impossible until it`s achieved.

Nothing's impossible until it's achieved.

Nothing's impossible until it's achieved.

Age cannot cage our dreams and goals.

Age cannot cage our dreams and goals.

Age cannot cage our dreams and goals.

Age cannot cage our dreams and goals.

Goals shape you, reaching them transforms.

Goals shape you, reaching them transforms.

Goals shape you, reaching them transforms.

Goals shape you, reaching them transforms.

Fear guards the door to your desires.

Fear guards the door to your desires.

Fear guards the door to your desires.

Fear guards the door to your desires.

Today`s doubts are your tomorrow`s barriers.

Today`s doubts are your tomorrow`s barriers .

Today's doubts are your tomorrow's barriers.

Today's doubts are your tomorrow's barriers.

Make the most of now, with what you have.

Make the most of now, with what you have.

Make the most of now, with what you have.

Make the most of now, with what you have.

To be great, start. Action breeds triumph.

To be great, start. Action breeds triumph.

To be great, start. Action breeds triumph.

To be great, start. Action breeds triumph.

Challenges illuminate the path to personal triumph.

Challenges illuminate the path to personal triumph.

Challenges illuminate the path to personal triumph.

Challenges illuminate the path to personal triumph.

Grit is the bridge between struggle and success.

Grit is the bridge between struggle and success.

Grit is the bridge between struggle and success.

Grit is the bridge between struggle and success.

Hope is the spark that ignites the flame of progress.

Hope is the spark that ignites the flame of progress.

Hope is the spark that ignites the flame of progress.

Hope is the spark that ignites the flame of progress.

True strength is forged in the fires of perseverance.

True strength is forged in the fires of perseverance.

True strength is forged in the fires of perseverance.

True strength is forged in the fires of perseverance.

Vision without action is merely a dream realized.

Vision without action is merely a dream realized.

Vision without action is merely a dream realized.

Vision without action is merely a dream realized.

Become who you are.

Become who you are.

Become who you are.

Become who you are.

Without music, life would be a mistake.

Without music, life would be a mistake.

Without music, life would be a mistake.

Without music, life would be a mistake.

He who has a why in life can tolerate almost any how.

He who has a why in life can tolerate almost any how.

He who has a why in life can tolerate almost any how.

He who has a why in life can tolerate almost any how.

There are no beautiful surfaces without a terrible depth

There are no beautiful surfaces without a terrible depth

There are no beautiful surfaces without a terrible depth

There are no beautiful surfaces without a terrible depth

There are no facts, only interpretations.

There are no facts, only interpretations.

There are no facts, only interpretations.

There are no facts, only interpretations.

What does not kill me, makes me stronger.

What does not kill me, makes me stronger.

What does not kill me, makes me stronger.

What does not kill me, makes me stronger.

Creativity is the color of the soul's true voice.

Creativity is the color of the soul's true voice.

Creativity is the color of the soul's true voice.

Creativity is the color of the soul's true voice.

Every step forward is a victory over yesterday.

Every step forward is a victory over yesterday.

Every step forward is a victory over yesterday.

Every step forward is a victory over yesterday.

Joy is found not in finishing an activity but in doing it.

Joy is found not in finishing an activity but in doing it.

Joy is found not in finishing an activity but in doing it.

Joy is found not in finishing an activity but in doing it.

Courage is the companion of those who dare to dream.

Courage is the companion of those who dare to dream.

Courage is the companion of those who dare to dream.

Courage is the companion of those who dare to dream.

Part 4
Short Poems

Track the dotted poems and then write the poems on your own.

In the heart`s quiet, whispers of dreams awaken.

In the heart`s quiet, whispers of dreams awaken.

In the heart's quiet, whispers of dreams awaken.

In the heart's quiet, whispers of dreams awaken.

Dawn`s light breaks, painting hope on the horizon.

Dawn`s light breaks, painting hope on the horizon .

Dawn's light breaks, painting hope on the horizon.

Dawn's light breaks, painting hope on the horizon.

Stars whisper secrets to the night`s velvet cloak.

Stars whisper secrets to the night`s velvet cloak.

Stars whisper secrets to the night's velvet cloak.

Stars whisper secrets to the night's velvet cloak.

Waves caress shores in an endless dance of love.

Waves caress shores in an endless dance of love.

Waves caress shores in an endless dance of love.

Waves caress shores in an endless dance of love.

Winds carry songs of the untold across the world.

Winds carry songs of the untold across the world.

Winds carry songs of the untold across the world.

Winds carry songs of the untold across the world.

Mountains stand, guardians of time`s silent story.

Mountains stand, guardians of time`s silent story.

Mountains stand, guardians of time's silent story.

Mountains stand, guardians of time's silent story.

Flowers bloom, nature`s tender kiss on the earth.

Flowers bloom, nature`s tender kiss on the earth.

Flowers bloom, nature's tender kiss on the earth.

Flowers bloom, nature's tender kiss on the earth.

Rain`s gentle touch revives the thirsting ground.

Rain`s gentle touch revives the thirsting ground.

Rain's gentle touch revives the thirsting ground.

Rain's gentle touch revives the thirsting ground.

Leaves rustle, a symphony in the forest`s heart.

Leaves rustle, a symphony in the forest`s heart.

Leaves rustle, a symphony in the forest's heart.

Leaves rustle, a symphony in the forest's heart.

Snowflakes dance, winter`s delicate ballet begins.

Snowflakes dance, winter`s delicate ballet begins.

Snowflakes dance, winter's delicate ballet begins.

Snowflakes dance, winter's delicate ballet begins.

Sunsets paint the sky in hues of fiery promise.

Sunsets paint the sky in hues of fiery promise.

Sunsets paint the sky in hues of fiery promise.

Sunsets paint the sky in hues of fiery promise.

Night`s embrace holds the world in quiet peace.

Night`s embrace holds the world in quiet peace.

Night's embrace holds the world in quiet peace.

Night's embrace holds the world in quiet peace.

Rivers sing melodies of journeys to the sea.

Rivers sing melodies of journeys to the sea.

Rivers sing melodies of journeys to the sea.

Rivers sing melodies of journeys to the sea.

Birds soar, tracing dreams against the blue sky.

Birds soar, tracing dreams against the blue sky.

Birds soar, tracing dreams against the blue sky.

Birds soar, tracing dreams against the blue sky.

Stars` glow whispers of infinity`s quiet beauty.

Stars` glow whispers of infinity`s quiet beauty.

Stars' glow whispers of infinity's quiet beauty.

Stars' glow whispers of infinity's quiet beauty.

Moonlight bathes the earth in a silver serene glow.

Moonlight bathes the earth in a silver serene glow.

Moonlight bathes the earth in a silver serene glow.

Moonlight bathes the earth in a silver serene glow.

Autumn`s canvas brings the dance of changing leaves.

Autumn`s canvas brings the dance of changing leaves.

Autumn's canvas brings the dance of changing leaves.

Autumn's canvas brings the dance of changing leaves.

Silence speaks volumes in the language of the soul.

Silence speaks volumes in the language of the soul.

Silence speaks volumes in the language of the soul.

Silence speaks volumes in the language of the soul.

The horizon calls, a promise of adventures new.

The horizon calls, a promise of adventures new.

The horizon calls, a promise of adventures new.

The horizon calls, a promise of adventures new.

Time whispers tales in the ruins of the ancient.

Time whispers tales in the ruins of the ancient.

Time whispers tales in the ruins of the ancient.

Time whispers tales in the ruins of the ancient.

Echoes of laughter linger in the forgotten halls.

Echoes of laughter linger in the forgotten halls.

Echoes of laughter linger in the forgotten halls.

Echoes of laughter linger in the forgotten halls.

Frost sketches fine art on winter window panes.

Frost sketches fine art on winter window panes.

Frost sketches fine art on winter window panes.

Frost sketches fine art on winter window panes.

Clouds drift lazily, sketching dreams in the sky.

Clouds drift lazily, sketching dreams in the sky.

Clouds drift lazily, sketching dreams in the sky.

Clouds drift lazily, sketching dreams in the sky.

Oceans roar their timeless tales to sandy shores.

Oceans roar their timeless tales to sandy shores.

Oceans roar their timeless tales to sandy shores.

Oceans roar their timeless tales to sandy shores.

Gentle dusk settles, cloaking the day in tranquility.

Gentle dusk settles, cloaking the day in tranquility.

Gentle dusk settles, cloaking the day in tranquility.

Gentle dusk settles, cloaking the day in tranquility.

Candlelight flickers, casting stories on the walls.

Candlelight flickers, casting stories on the walls.

Candlelight flickers, casting stories on the walls.

Candlelight flickers, casting stories on the walls.

Spring whispers growth with each new bloom`s burst.

Spring whispers growth with each new bloom`s burst.

Spring whispers growth with each new bloom's burst.

Spring whispers growth with each new bloom's burst.

Shadows dance on the walls under the moon`s watch.

Shadows dance on the walls under the moon`s watch.

Shadows dance on the walls under the moon's watch.

Shadows dance on the walls under the moon's watch.

Paths worn by footsteps telling stories of old.

Paths worn by footsteps telling stories of old.

Paths worn by footsteps telling stories of old.

Paths worn by footsteps telling stories of old.

Stars chart the course of silent celestial voyages.

Stars chart the course of silent celestial voyages.

Stars chart the course of silent celestial voyages.

Stars chart the course of silent celestial voyages.

Made in United States
Troutdale, OR
10/11/2024